Great Zimbabwe

digging
for the past

BRIAN FAGAN
General Editor

Great Zimbabwe

Martin Hall and Rebecca Stefoff

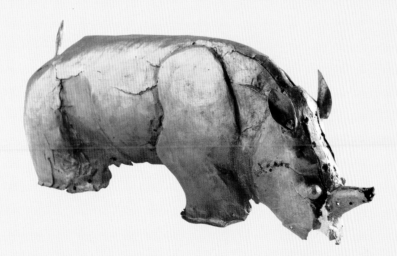

OXFORD
UNIVERSITY PRESS

OXFORD
UNIVERSITY PRESS

Oxford University Press, Inc., publishes works that further
Oxford University's objective of excellence
in research, scholarship, and education.

Oxford New York
Auckland Cape Town Dar es Salaam Hong Kong Karachi
Kuala Lumpur Madrid Melbourne Mexico City Nairobi
New Delhi Shanghai Taipei Toronto

With offices in
Argentina Austria Brazil Chile Czech Republic France Greece
Guatemala Hungary Italy Japan Poland Portugal Singapore
South Korea Switzerland Thailand Turkey Ukraine Vietnam

Copyright © 2006 by Oxford University Press, Inc.

Published by Oxford University Press, Inc.
198 Madison Avenue, New York, New York 10016
www.oup.com

Oxford is a registered trademark of Oxford University Press

Library of Congress Cataloging-in-Publication Data

Hall, Martin
  Great Zimbabwe : digging for the past / Martin Hall and Rebecca Stefoff.— 1st ed.
    p. cm. — (Digging for the past)
  Includes bibliographical references and index.
  ISBN-13: 978-0-19-515773-4
  ISBN-10: 0-19-515773-7
  1. Great Zimbabwe (Extinct city)—Juvenile literature. 2. Shona (African people)—
Zimbabwe—Great Zimbabwe (Extinct city)—History—Juvenile literature. I. Stefoff,
Rebecca, 1951- II. Title. III. Series.
  DT3025.G84H35 2005
  968.91'01—dc22
                                                              2005014607

Printing number: 9 8 7 6 5 4 3 2 1

Printed in China
on acid-free paper

Cover: *In 1978, archaeologists excavated a sunken passage that connects the Great Enclosure to other nearby ruins on the Valley floor of the site.*

Frontispiece: *A team of archaelogists excavate the remains of a hut inside the Great Enclosure, the largest African stone ruin south of the Sahara Desert.*

Picture Credits: Archiv des Justus Perthes Verlages Gotha: 20; Bildarchiv Preußischer Kulturbesitz: 13; British Academy: 21; By Permission of the British Library Add. 5415 A: 12; © The Trustees of the British Museum: 32; C/Z HARRIS LTD.: 41 (bottom); Photograph courtesy of Sian Tiley, the Mapungubwe Museum, University of Pretoria: 2, 35; Martin Hall: Cover (background), 1, 10, 22 (left), 41 (top), 44, 45; Hauptstaatsarchiv Stuttgart, All Rights Reserved: 14 (right); Eugenia Herbert: 8, 22 (right), 26; Iziko Museums of Cape Town, photographer: Cecil Kortjie: 27 (left), 29 (bottom); Library of Congress, LC-USZ62-97831: 34; National Archives of Zimbabwe: 16, 19, 23, 27 (right), 31, 40 (bottom); H. Hall / National Geographic Image Collection: 39; Walter Meayers Edwards / National Geographic Image Collection: 33; Courtesy of the National Museums and Monuments of Zimbabwe: Cover (inset), 2, 14 (left), 24, 28 (top and bottom), 29 (top), 30; Map Division, The New York Public Library, Astor, Lenox and Tilden Foundations: 9; Department of Special Collections, Stanford University Libraries: 37; Photo courtesy of The University of Arizona: 25; Zimbabwe Tourist Office: 17, 18.

Contents

Where and When

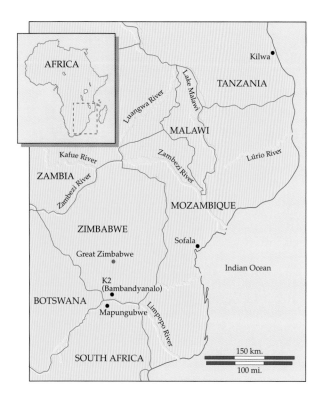

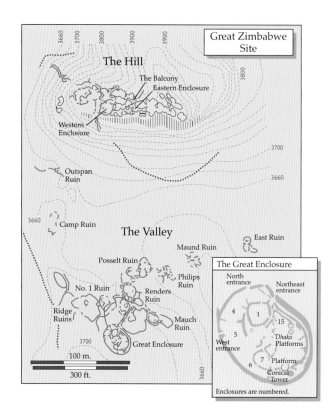

Early History

1250 ▶
Mapungubwe is well established as a regional state in southeastern Africa

◀ **1300**
Construction of stone walls begins at Great Zimbabwe

1350 ▶
Great Zimbabwe, leading Shona power, is part of widespread trade network

◀ **1450**
Construction ends at Great Zimbabwe

1500s ▶
Inhabitants slowly abandon Great Zimbabwe; successor states Torwa and Rozwi rise to power

◀ **1505**
Portuguese seize port of Kilwa on Indian Ocean coast

1512 ▶
Portuguese search for gold in southeastern Africa, disrupting African trade network

Archaeological History

1609	◀ João de Santos links the African stone buildings to King Solomon and the Queen of Sheba
1871	◀ Karl Mauch locates ruins of Great Zimbabwe
1899	◀ Mashonaland (later Rhodesia) comes under control of the financier Cecil Rhodes
1901–1904	◀ Richard N. Hall digs at Great Zimbabwe
1905	◀ David Randall-MacIver declares Great Zimbabwe African in origin
1931	◀ Gertrude Caton-Thompson confirms African origins of Great Zimbabwe
1958	◀ Radiocarbon dating of Great Zimbabwe begins
1960s	◀ White government of Rhodesia denies Great Zimbabwe's African origin
1980	◀ Black majority rule begins in former Rhodesia, renamed Zimbabwe
1986	◀ UNESCO names Great Zimbabwe a World Heritage Site

1

Encounters

Stone walls crown the Hill, a section of Great Zimbabwe that looms steeply above the rest of the site.

In the 14th and 15th centuries, the city of Kilwa on the East African coast was a thriving trade center with as many as 20,000 inhabitants. The people of Kilwa traded cloth from the local weaving industry for gold from the African interior, glass beads from India, and fine pottery from China. Dhows, triangular-sailed ships that crossed the Indian Ocean, crowded Kilwa's harbor. But one day in 1505, a different sort of fleet arrived. Its 22 European ships carried 1,500 soldiers commanded by Viceroy Francisco de Almeida of Portugal, under orders from his king to seize Kilwa.

East Africans had seen such ships before. Just six years earlier the Portuguese navigator Vasco da Gama, the first European to sail around the tip of Africa, had landed at several East African ports on his way to India. Returning to Portugal, he had told the king about the prosperity and safe harbors of these trading ports. Portugal wanted some of those ports to expand its trading empire.

After Almeida's fleet arrived, the sheikh who ruled Kilwa fled. The Portuguese replaced him with a sheikh they could control, then set about tightening their grip on Kilwa and other ports, especially Sofala to the south, in what is now Mozambique. Their arrival launched an era of European conquest and colonization in the region. It also began the Europeans' long and frustrating quest for the mythical civilizations they thought lay hidden in the African interior. The Europeans never found the places they sought, but in time they came upon the lasting monument of a former African civilization: the massive city of Great Zimbabwe. With masterfully built stone walls snaking across a rocky ridge and walls and towers dotting the plain below, Great Zimbabwe would become a source of mysteries

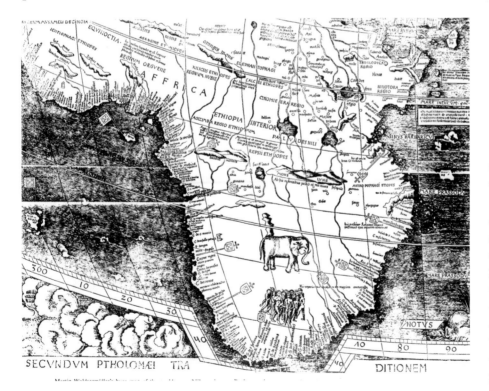

On this detail from a German world map of 1507, the African coast is lined with place-names, but the interior remains mysteriously blank except for some fanciful images and geographic features. For centuries, European maps of Africa's interior were based on rumors, ancient geographies, and plain old imagination.

This narrow passage is sandwiched between the inner and outer walls of one of Great Zimbabwe's most important ruins, the Great Enclosure. At the end of the passage lies the Conical Tower.

and controversies for those who heard about it and explored it in years to come.

The Portuguese took a keen interest in the gold from the African interior that reached the coastal markets. They were eager to discover—and, if possible, control—the sources of that gold. In 1512, António Fernandes led an expedition from Sofala in search of a rumored gold-producing region called Monomotapa. A few other expeditions followed during the 16th and early 17th centuries. Portuguese soldiers and adventurers, sometimes burdened with heavy armor, toiled inland through the African heat, battling disease as well as the local warriors who tried to defend their homelands from the intruders.

These explorers and native traders passed on tales suggesting that somewhere in the interior was a kingdom rich in gold, where kings lived in stone houses. In 1552, a Portuguese historian named João de Barros described a "square fortress, of masonry within and without, built of stones of marvelous size" and a nearby stone tower, both built without mortar. The entire place, according to Barros, was "royal property" and "guarded by a nobleman." Writing around the same time, another historian named Damião de Goes claimed that the king of Monomotapa "keeps great state, and is served on bended knees with reverence." A century later, an English geographer named John Ogilvie wrote that the palace of

Monomotapa was "covered over with plates of gold." These stories were inspired by the myth of Prester John, whom Europeans imagined to be a rich and powerful Christian emperor living on the fringe of the known world. Whenever European explorers heard of a mighty kingdom beyond the horizon, they thought they were on the verge of finding him at last.

The Portuguese in Sofala never found the wealthy realms they imagined. A few adventurers, however, did come into brief contact with Mutapa and Torwa, interior states that mined and traded gold and built impressive stone structures. Writing of these encounters, Portuguese historians speculated that the large stone buildings and cities in the interior of southeastern Africa had been built long ago as outposts of ancient cultures mentioned in the Bible. In 1609, João de Santos, who had been a missionary in Mutapa, wrote a book linking the African stone buildings with old biblical stories about King Solomon and the Queen of Sheba. Santos's idea proved long-lived.

Mutapa and Torwa were the most recent in a series of states that had risen to power on the Zimbabwe Plateau, a rolling highland plain between the Zambezi and Limpopo Rivers. The population centers of Mutapa and Torwa ranged from settlements of just a few families to good-sized regional cities. The largest and most impressive was the

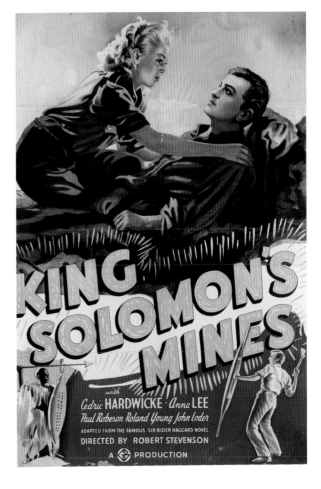

Set in a lost African city linked to the biblical king Solomon, the 1885 adventure novel King Solomon's Mines *captured one of the myths about Great Zimbabwe's origins. This poster is for the 1937 movie, one of several film versions.*

In 1558, the Portuguese cartographer Diogo Homem made this map of the Indian Ocean and East Africa. Depicted on a throne facing the African coast is Prester John, the imaginary ruler for whom European explorers would still be searching more than a century later.

city that the Portuguese referred to as Symbaoe and that we now call Great Zimbabwe.

The few Portuguese who reached Great Zimbabwe arrived after its 300-year history as Africa's largest city south of the Sahara Desert had come to a close. By that time, Great Zimbabwe no longer occupied a central place in the affairs of the African peoples of the Zimbabwe Plateau, and to the outside world it was only a fading rumor. As the centuries passed, European mapmakers who remembered old tales sometimes drew cities or castles on their maps of southeastern Africa, but these were as fanciful as the images of sea monsters and whirlpools that also adorned their work.

By the 19th century, European missionaries and settlers were moving north onto the Zimbabwe Plateau from what is now South Africa.

A German missionary named Alexander Merensky gathered and passed on stories about a vast, ruined stone city in the interior—a ruin that he thought must be Ophir, a city mentioned in the biblical accounts of Solomon and Sheba. Karl Mauch, a German geologist seeking fortune and fame in Africa, listened eagerly to Merensky's theories. In 1871, Mauch went looking for the ruins of "old Monomotapa or Ophir," as he wrote in his diary.

Tall, heavily bearded, clad in a suit of antelope hide that he made himself, and carrying a large umbrella, several guns, and more than 50 pounds of gear (including books and painting equipment), Mauch trudged into a territory called Mashonaland. There he met another German, an ivory dealer named Adam Renders, who said he knew of the ruins. With the help of Renders and a local guide, Mauch found Great Zimbabwe. To Mauch's disappointment, he found no gold or jewels. Nor did he find written inscriptions that might offer clues about the city's builders or its history. Still, Mauch had no doubt that the ruins were those of the biblical city Ophir. He cut a sliver of wood from a beam in one ruin. Thinking that the wood was cedar, he decided that the beam must have come from Lebanon, mentioned in the Bible as Solomon's source of cedar. From this shaky starting point, Mauch's imagination made another bold leap, and he identified the ruin as the Queen of Sheba's palace.

Mauch returned to Germany, where his announcement revived the old idea that far-ranging Near Eastern people had been active in southern Africa centuries earlier. This idea appealed to late 19th-century Europeans for several reasons. They were familiar with the monumental stone architecture of the Near East, such as the

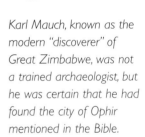

Karl Mauch, known as the modern "discoverer" of Great Zimbabwe, was not a trained archaeologist, but he was certain that he had found the city of Ophir mentioned in the Bible.

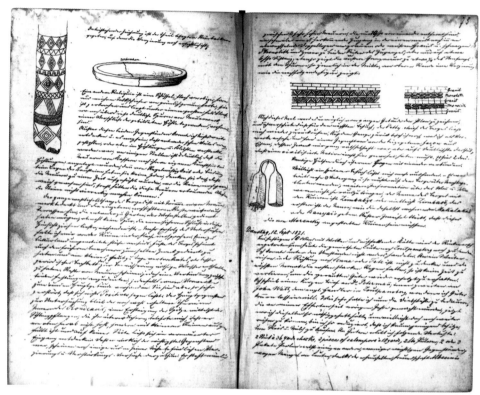

The iron double gong that Karl Mauch found and sketched at Great Zimbabwe has been dated to the 14th or 15th century. In these pages from his notebook (right) Mauch illustrated patterns of stonework and decorative carvings, as well as a cracked bowl and this gong.

Egyptians' Great Pyramid, and to many it seemed logical to link the only stone ruins south of the Sahara Desert with these well-known ancient builders. The primary reason, though, stemmed from racial prejudice. Europeans were colonizing southern Africa, seizing land from native peoples such as the Shona and Zulu. To justify their actions, white politicians, soldiers, and settlers needed to believe that they were superior to the black Africans. They could not accept that black Africans, whom they were accustomed to regarding as "savages," had built the large, well-made stone structures. As word of Mauch's find spread, treasure hunters descended on the ruins to dig for gold. They destroyed archaeological evidence, littered the area with broken liquor bottles and old boots, and were rewarded with small amounts of gold.

In 1890, Mashonaland came under the control of Cecil Rhodes, a British financier who organized the British South Africa Company to establish a colony there. Fascinated with Great Zimbabwe, Rhodes sponsored new excavations of the site, aimed at unearthing both treasure and knowledge. Theodore Bent—who had the support of two leading British scientific organizations, the Royal Geographic Society and the British Association for the Advancement of Science—led the first "scientific" study. Bent had specialized in the study of the Phoenicians, an ancient Mediterranean and Near Eastern people. He thought at first that the African interior had little to offer an archaeologist. The ruins of Great Zimbabwe, he claimed, were African and not very ancient. Then he came upon some of the most striking artifacts ever found at the site: large birds carved from stone, sitting atop stone pillars. These reminded Bent of ancient Mediterranean and Near Eastern artifacts. Soon he had decided that the ruins were not African after all. Arabs, he claimed, had built them—but he also detected, perhaps not surprisingly, a Phoenician influence.

A journalist named Richard N. Hall, whom Rhodes's company placed in charge of the ruins, wrote the next chapter in the mythology of Great Zimbabwe. Hall worked there from 1901 to 1904—to the lasting regret of later experts. His methods were forceful and destructive. In the course of "restoring" the ruins to what he thought had been their former appearance, Hall cleared away layer upon layer of deposits that would have given much valuable information to careful scientific researchers. In his report to Rhodes, Hall echoed Bent's verdict, saying that one of "the more

The Eastern Enclosure of the Hill as it appeared in the late 19th century, around the time of Theodore Bent's "scientific" study. Much of the walling from this part of the site no longer survives.

The Eastern Enclosure of the Hill as it appeared in the late 19th century, around the time of Theodore Bent's "scientific" study. Much of the walling from this part of the site no longer survives.

civilized races of the ancient world," Arabs or Near Easterners, had built Great Zimbabwe.

Thanks to people such as Bent and Hall, the non-African origin of the ruins became established as their official history. As early as 1905, however, an archaeologist named David Randall-MacIver lifted the veils of myth and racism. After close examination of the ruins, Randall-MacIver announced that Great Zimbabwe was "unquestionably African in every detail." Randall-MacIver was right, but the white colonial establishment rejected his views. Most people were simply not ready to accept the idea that a skilled and powerful civilization had arisen in black Africa. They found other theories more attractive—and there were plenty of them. Various theories gave credit for Great Zimbabwe to ancient Egyptians, shipwrecked Vikings, and even the mythical "lost civilization" of Atlantis.

Gertrude Caton-Thompson, a skilled archaeologist whom the British Association for the Advancement of Science sent to Great Zimbabwe in 1929 to examine the site anew, filed letters about the most absurd crackpot theories under "insane." Caton-Thompson's careful study employed stratigraphy, one of the cornerstones of modern archaeology. Stratigraphy is the study of layers of soil. Deeper layers are older than the layers above them. By meticulously measuring the depth of everything found at a site, archaeologists can develop a chronology, or sequence of events across time, for the site.

Caton-Thompson concluded in *Zimbabwe Culture*, her report on her investigation, that Great Zimbabwe was the relic of "a native civilization" of "originality and amazing industry." Although she suggested that Arab or Near Eastern traders who visited the coastal cities of East Africa might have influenced the site's African builders, her main finding was clear: Great Zimbabwe was African, and it was much more recent than the ancient cultures of biblical legend. Still, the old colonial myths about Great Zimbabwe's non-African origins have lingered for years. All experts, however, now accept the scientific evidence that Africans built and occupied the sites that gave the modern nation of Zimbabwe its name, which comes from the Shona phrase *dzimba woye*, meaning "honored houses," or *dzimba dza mabwe*, "houses of stone."

Great Zimbabwe's massive, well-constructed stone walls and towers made a powerful impression on the first Europeans to see them. The Conical Tower, seen here, is one of the most distinctive features of the site.

2

Houses of Stone

Seen from atop the Hill, the Valley ruins spread across the landscape. No one is certain how many people lived at Great Zimbabwe, but one archaeologist has estimated its peak population at 18,000.

Great Zimbabwe's name refers to houses of stone, but the site contains no houses in the ordinary sense of the word. Instead, massive stone walls snake across the landscape, enclosing areas both large and small. Piles of tumbled stones mark the places where other walls once stood. These enclosures and walls are the remains of the city that once dominated the Zimbabwe Plateau.

Great Zimbabwe is in south-central Zimbabwe, 17 miles southeast of the town of Masvingo, in an area where climate and resources were favorable to settlers. The site is more than 3,000 feet above sea level, cooler than the hot coastal plain. It is free of the tsetse fly, which in many other parts of Africa infects both humans and livestock with disease-causing parasites. The plateau's grassy plains were ideal for cattle grazing, and its scattered trees and forests provided the builders of Great Zimbabwe with timber for fuel and construction. Granite hills and rock outcroppings yielded gold, iron, copper, and tin.

Equally important was the granite itself, which cracks in a process that geologists call exfoliation. The change in temperature between the warm days and chilly nights causes the rock to split into natural building blocks, flat-sided slabs between three and seven inches thick. The people of the plateau learned to speed up the production of these slabs by heating the surface of the granite with fire and then cooling it suddenly with water.

Many thousands of stones went into the building of Great Zimbabwe. The sprawling site covers about 1,800 acres, which archaeologists have divided into three general areas: the Hill, the Valley, and the Outer City.

The first sight that greets visitors is the Hill. Its steep sides rise 260 feet above the surrounding landscape, and its summit is crowned with many rock formations. Walls run between natural outcrops and boulders, creating a network of small passageways and enclosures. Like all structures at Great Zimbabwe, these are open to the sky. Archaeologists have found no evidence that the site's stone structures had roofs. Instead, the enclosures

This round house built of mud-plastered poles with a cone-shaped thatched roof is typical of the traditional Shona homes that most likely filled the stone enclosures of Great Zimbabwe.

are thought to have contained small thatched-roof structures made of *dhaka*, a type of soil containing clay and gravel that is a common African building material. Large pits near Great Zimbabwe provided *dhaka* for the site.

At one end of the Hill is a walled area called the Eastern Enclosure that once held many monoliths, or standing stones and pillars. The tops of some of these pillars were carved as birds, which may have represented individual rulers of Great Zimbabwe. From the Eastern Enclosure a narrow passage climbs between boulders up to the Balcony, the highest enclosure on the Hill. It offers a view down over the Eastern Enclosure and, below it, the spreading Valley.

About 200 feet away is the larger Western Enclosure, ringed by two curving stone walls that are 26 feet at their highest point and

Karl Mauch painted this watercolor of the Hill at Great Zimbabwe, which he called an "acropolis." At one time archaeologists used this term for any steep hill bearing ancient ruins; the best-known acropolis is located in Athens, Greece.

16 feet at their widest. These walls, like many at Great Zimbabwe, are really two walls in one—an inner and an outer wall made of slabs laid in courses, or layers, with loose stone, dirt, and gravel filling the space between them. The slabs fit snugly together, without the use of mortar. Monoliths and turrets once stood at intervals along the top of the Western Enclosure's walls. Within the enclosure, excavators have found layers of *dhaka* floors, broken pottery, and other signs that the site was continuously occupied for many years. Most archaeologists today believe that the Hill was the seat of royal power in Great Zimbabwe. The Western Enclosure probably housed kings or chiefs. The Eastern Enclosure may have been a religious or ritual place where sacred emblems—symbolic objects such as the monoliths and carved birds—were displayed. South of the Hill lies the Valley. It contains about a dozen enclosures ringed or partly ringed by stone walls. Several major archaeological projects at Great Zimbabwe have focused on these ruins. In 1929, Gertrude Caton-Thompson methodically excavated one of them and correctly concluded that it was African in origin and that it dated from the medieval, not the ancient, period. In another enclosure, which Hall excavated in 1903, was a great hoard of artifacts.

The Valley enclosures tell a story in stonework of Great Zimbabwe's rise and decline. The architect Anthony Whitty studied these enclosures in the 1950s and identified three main construction styles, each from a different phase of Great Zimbabwe's history. The oldest phase features crude stonework, untrimmed stones laid in irregular or uneven courses. This phase probably began around

Gertrude Caton-Thompson had done significant research at several sites in Egypt before the British Association for the Advancement of Science sent her to Great Zimbabwe in 1929. She proved beyond a doubt that Great Zimbabwe was of African origin.

The early builders of Great Zimbabwe laid stones of various sizes together to form irregular walls (left). A bit later, in the mid-14th century, more accomplished builders trimmed and matched stones to form even rows and built decorative bands into the walls (right).

1300. During the second phase, in the 14th century, Great Zimbabwe's builders produced their finest walls, using stones that had been carefully trimmed to fit neatly together and laying them in even courses, sometimes setting them in decorative patterns such as zigzags or chevrons, a V-shaped design. During the third phase, in the 15th century, the quality of stonework declined for unknown reasons. Walls were made of irregularly sized stones, sometimes piled crudely together or forcefully wedged into place.

The focal point of the Valley is the largest African stone ruin south of the Sahara Desert. Known as the Great Enclosure, this oval space is surrounded by an 800-foot-long wall, 32 feet high and 17 feet thick in places. The massive wall is thicker at the bottom than at the top, making it very stable. Along part of the enclosure, an inner wall runs parallel to the main wall, with a deep, narrow passageway between the two. This passageway leads to the Great Enclosure's most striking feature: the Conical Tower. This solid, cone-shaped structure is 30 feet high and 18 feet across at the base. The Great Enclosure also contains a number of smaller enclosures and *dhaka* platforms.

The purpose of the Great Enclosure, like much else about Great Zimbabwe, has been widely debated. Various investigators have identified it as a temple, the residence of the king's wives, or a private community set aside for members of the royal court or other elite citizens. The archaeologist Thomas Huffman has suggested that the Great Enclosure may have been a school where young women underwent training and rituals to prepare them for initiation into adult society. He bases this suggestion on the fact that some African cultures in the region maintain such schools today, and have done so for generations.

Beyond the Valley enclosures is the Outer City, the least-known part of the site. Once the densely crowded home of most of Great Zimbabwe's inhabitants, today it consists mostly of the remains of *dhaka* huts, with occasional stone enclosures scattered about the surrounding countryside. Based on his examination of the site, Huffman has estimated that Great Zimbabwe could have housed as many as 18,000 people at its peak, making it a true urban center in the midst of medieval southern Africa.

When Europeans encountered Great Zimbabwe in the

This travel poster from 1938, featuring the Conical Tower and a stone bird, promotes the myth that Great Zimbabwe had some connection with the biblical Queen of Sheba. An African man kneels before the queen's ghostly figure, reflecting the racist view of Great Zimbabwe's non-African origins.

Radiocarbon Reality

Some of the most heated debates about Great Zimbabwe concerned the age of the ruins. Those who insisted that ancient Egyptians, Phoenicians, or other non-Africans had built the site claimed that Great Zimbabwe was thousands of years old. In the mid-20th century, a new archaeological tool helped end these speculations and opened the way to a more accurate understanding of Great Zimbabwe's history.

That tool was radiocarbon dating. All organic, or living, matter contains small quantities of radioactive carbon, or radiocarbon. When a living organism dies, the radiocarbon in its tissue begins to decay at a fixed rate. By measuring the amount of radiocarbon remaining in a sample of ancient organic matter, then comparing that figure with the amount found in a sample of comparable living matter, scientists can determine how much radiocarbon has decayed in the sample—in

Radiocarbon dating can be applied to any organic material, including human remains, such as this partial skeleton excavated at Great Zimbabwe in 1991. The body had been buried between two stone walls of a ruin northwest of the main site's Hill complex.

other words, how long ago the sample died. Archaeologists use radiocarbon dating to discover the ages of human and animal remains and of wooden structures.

A team of scientists at the University of Chicago developed radiocarbon dating in the years after World War II. They tested it first on samples of wood from an ancient Egyptian tomb the age of which was already known from other sources. After the method had been shown to be reliable, archaeologists began using it to measure the age of all kinds of materials, including hair, leather, wall paintings, blood, textiles, pottery, wood, bone, and the dried remains of insects, grain, and wine. They also broadened their investigations beyond Egypt to other Mediterranean sites and then to archaeological sites around the world.

A laboratory worker uses a microscope to measure a small sample of organic matter—which can include bone, wood, charcoal, or cloth—from an ancient artifact. Using carbon dating, scientists can determine the age of such samples.

Beginning in 1958, the archaeologist Keith Robinson applied radiocarbon dating to Great Zimbabwe, testing timber poles he found while excavating a trench in the Western Enclosure. He obtained a date of 1065 CE (plus or minus 150 years). This means that the trees from which the poles were made grew between 915 and 1215 CE, although the poles may have been used in construction at a later date. Robinson's work was important because it set the building of the major ruins within the past thousand or so years, much more recent than the misty depths of antiquity. More recently, Great Zimbabwe has been firmly dated from a series of radiocarbon samples that have been carefully matched with one another and cross-checked for accuracy. As a result of this application of modern scientific techniques, the age of Great Zimbabwe is no longer in doubt. The city was built between 1300 and 1450 CE.

The wall surrounding the Great Enclosure is 800 feet long. It displays several characteristic features of Great Zimbabwe's architecture, including rounded corners and curved steps.

late 19th century, they felt an awe, inspired by their mistaken ideas about the "mysterious" and "exotic" origins of the ruins. Modern archaeology has given us a more accurate view of Great Zimbabwe's origins and history, but the site remains as impressive and as ever, a massive memorial to an African past that is still being uncovered. The Zimbabwean government administers Great Zimbabwe as a national monument, and in 1986 the United Nations Educational, Scientific, and Cultural Organization (UNESCO) named Great Zimbabwe a World Heritage Site in recognition of its unique and valuable place in cultural and archaeological history.

3

Reading the Evidence

W hat was life like for the people of
Great Zimbabwe? How did they
work, worship, and organize their
society? The Great Zimbabwe people left no written
records, so archaeologists look to other sources for
information about their lives. Two of the most important
sources are the physical objects that the Great Zimbabweans left
behind and the stories that their modern descendants tell.

Some physical objects found at Great Zimbabwe are rare and
special artifacts that probably had great importance during the city's
heyday. Many are the ordinary relics of everyday life, such as
garbage, pottery, and tools. Animal bones, for example, have drawn
the attention of archaeozoologists, specialists in the animal life
associated with archaeological sites. They study the kinds of animals
found at a site, the number of each kind, and when possible, the
date and condition of the remains. The remains at Great Zimbabwe
and nearby sites reveal that cattle were the basis of the economy.
Cattle were more than food—they also served as a form of wealth
and a sign of status. People in outlying, low-status settlements
such as villages and farms hunted for wild game to supplement

*The parade of animals—
baboons, a dog, a bird, and
zebras—on this fragment
of a soapstone bowl (left)
is one of the most elabo-
rate decorative carvings
yet found among the arti-
facts of Great Zimbabwe.
A wooden bowl (right)
bears a carved crocodile.
Both bowls were found in
the 1890s.*

their diet of grain. They also kept cattle and other livestock, but the bones from the best cuts of meat have only been found within the larger *madzimbabwe*, or stone enclosures. It appears that the ordinary folk did not consume the prime cattle but rather turned them over to the elites—the powerful and privileged classes—who lived in the *madzimbabwe*.

Archaeologists also learn much from artifacts, humanmade objects such as utensils and artworks. Pots are an important and useful kind of artifact—not only do they offer insight into how they might have been used in everyday life, but they can often be dated by stylistic features such as shape, decoration, or material. In spite of the reckless and destructive methods of early excavators, Great Zimbabwe has yielded many examples of pottery, both whole pots and the broken pieces known as potsherds. Great Zimbabwe pots are round and fall into two general types. Most are between 9 and 12 inches across, with short, slightly narrow necks, some with lids. The others are much larger, with three or four times the capacity of the smaller pots. The archaeologist Peter S. Garlake points out in his book *Great Zimbabwe* that the smaller vessels are similar to those the Shona people, descendants of the Great Zimbabweans, use today for drinking. The larger ones resemble pots that the Shona use for brewing beer or storing food. All the Great Zimbabwe pots were formed from lengths of local clay, wound and coiled into shape and then baked in a wood fire.

Among the other everyday objects found at the site are hundreds of disks between one and two inches across, with small holes through their centers. Some are made of pottery, others of the

Artifacts such as an iron hoe blade (top) and a bronze spearhead (bottom) indicate that the people of Great Zimbabwe were skilled metalworkers. Both objects date from the 14th or 15th century.

Archaeologists on a 1987 expedition to Great Zimbabwe excavate an earthen floor, the last remains of a hut, or house, inside the Great Enclosure. Many areas of the site remain unexcavated, leaving open the possibility of future discoveries that will expand our knowledge of life at Great Zimbabwe.

smooth, shiny, grayish-green rock known as soapstone, which is fairly soft and easy to carve. Archaeologists do not know for certain what purpose these disks served. Some believe that they were spindle whorls, weights placed on the ends of spindle rods used to spin cotton fiber into thread; the Shona have been known to use similar disks for that purpose. Others have suggested that the Great Zimbabwean disks may have been game pieces or dice used in fortune telling. The site also contained many metalworkers' tools, pieces of iron ore, and objects such as arrowheads, ax heads, and hoe blades made of local iron, as well as iron, copper, gold, and bronze wire and beads. These finds show that the people of Great Zimbabwe practiced metalworking on a large scale.

Many stone disks have been found at Great Zimbabwe, and their purpose is a mystery. Some archaeologists think they may have been parts of devices used to spin thread; others have suggested that they were game pieces.

Many archaeologists think that Great Zimbabwe contributed gold and other metals to the Indian Ocean trade—not just metal but luxury items, such as gold and copper wire and beads, made by Great Zimbabwean artisans. Objects found at Great Zimbabwe show that the city was part of a far-reaching trade network. In 1903, Richard N. Hall found a varied collection of objects, some of which—such as painted glass from Syria and a small bowl from Iran—had originated far from the Zimbabwe Plateau. Hall's find also included many pieces of Chinese celadon ware, a type of pale-green pottery. Later, Gertrude Caton-Thompson found many small glass beads in a rubbish heap below the Western Enclosure.

Among Great Zimbabwe's best-known and most distinctive artifacts are the "Zimbabwe birds." Early investigators found seven

The unique birds of carved soapstone are Great Zimbabwe's best-known artifacts. In all, seven bird sculptures and part of an eighth have been found at the site.

soapstone sculptures of birds, and part of an eighth, at various parts of the site. Each bird is about 14 inches tall and sits atop a 3-foot column. Each has a unique design. Some are decorated with circles on their wings, others with zigzag patterns on their columns, or some other distinct feature. Nothing closely resembling these sculptures has been found at any other archaeological site, and their meaning cannot be known for certain. Thomas Huffman, however, thinks that the birds may have represented the spirits of Zimbabwe's kings, who were both political and religious figures. Huffman's interpretation of Great Zimbabwe draws upon the stories, legends, myths, and traditions—what researchers call the ethnography—of the Shona people. This approach views an ancient site through the lens of the modern culture that is most closely linked to it. Ethnography is a valuable tool that can offer many clues about how ancient people might have viewed the world and organized their lives. It has limitations, however. The stories that people tell change over time and do not always accurately report events. Archaeologists use the ethnographic approach cautiously, trying to draw on as many sources as possible for balance.

In the case of Great Zimbabwe, Huffman has proposed an interpretation of the site based on the beliefs and rituals of the present-day Venda people, who now live south of the Limpopo River. Huffman believes the

A Shona warrior photographed in the 1920s wears his hair in the same style described in 1560 by a European traveler to the region. Recognizing the Shona as the closest living relatives of the Great Zimbabwe people, some archaeologists have used their culture and legends to help them interpret Great Zimbabwe.

Venda people are closely related to the Shona builders of Great Zimbabwe. He also draws on the worldview revealed in Shona oral tradition. In the Shona religion, male and female symbols and spaces are kept separate. He also points out that paired male and female architectural sites and symbols are part of Venda culture. Huffman sees evidence of this division in the architecture of Great Zimbabwe, where doors, pathways, and towers often occur in pairs. To Huffman, certain structures—notably the Western Enclosure on the Hill and the Conical Tower in the Great Enclosure—display male symbols, such as monoliths and spears. Other structures, such as part of the Great Enclosure's wall and the Cleft Rock Enclosure on the Hill, display female symbols, including snakes and V-shaped stone patterns.

Not all agree with this interpretation. Zimbabwean scholar David Beach, for example, has argued that Huffman relies too much on recent Shona myths and that the Venda culture is not as similar to Great Zimbabwean culture as Huffman claims. Although ethnographic interpretations of Great Zimbabwe and the other stone enclosures of the Zimbabwe Plateau may never be as matter-of-fact as bones and potsherds, they open up new possibilities for envisioning the way the builders and inhabitants of these sites saw their world and their roles in it.

In addition to birds, the artists of Great Zimbabwe carved other figures from soapstone. This 16-inch-tall statue of a humanlike figure, unearthed at the site in 1923, was probably used in a religious ritual.

New Work at Great Zimbabwe

Great Zimbabwe is a living site. It continues to capture the attention of archaeologists and historians worldwide. Its well-deserved status as a United Nations Educational, Scientific and Cultural Organization (UNESCO) World Heritage Site ensures that measures to conserve and preserve its architecture receive constant attention.

One of the challenges that archaeologists face is that excavations in and of themselves destroy important aspects of evidence from the past. This is because the context in which things are found is all-important. Because Great Zimbabwe was seriously damaged by the plundering of early diggers, who shoveled away tons of deposits looking for evidence to support their favorite theories, archaeologists today are acutely aware of the need to preserve what is left. There have been no major excavations in recent years, and none are likely in the near future.

This does not mean that there has been no new work. Recent scholarship has focused on interpreting the existing evidence in light of the oral histories and traditions of Zimbabwe. Innocent Pikirayi, an archaeologist and professor of history at the University of Zimbabwe, has studied the evidence to learn about the origins and decline of early Zimbabwe.

Work such as this ensures that Great Zimbabwe will stay in the limelight. This attention poses a challenge for conservationists. How can the site be made accessible to more and more visitors while at the same time be preserved? In common with other World Heritage Sites, Great Zimbabwe needs both public support and professional care if it is to be preserved for future generations.

A Zimbabwean villager uses traditional musical instruments similar to those that may have been used by the people of Great Zimbabwe: panpipes, a ceremonial drum, leg rattles, and a mibra or thumb piano.

4

A Shona Empire

Richard N. Hall's team excavates the area in front of the Conical Tower in 1902. The raised platform around the tree shows the level of the ground before Hall began his "restoration"—revealing how much material he carted away and dumped, to the regret of later scientists.

Great Zimbabwe's massive stonework is a sign that the city was an important place with a sophisticated political and social system. Now that myths about the city's exotic origins have been swept away, archaeologists and historians have begun to draw its true story forth from the physical evidence found at the site and from the careful study of additional sources, such as old Portuguese accounts of trade and exploration and African oral traditions. As a result, a picture has emerged of Great Zimbabwe's place in the flow of history in southern Africa.

Before Great Zimbabwe, there was Mapungubwe. Like Great Zimbabwe, Mapungubwe was a city, the center of a vibrant culture.

Mapungubwe was strategically located in the valley of the Limpopo River south of Great Zimbabwe, commanding access to grazing lands and trade routes. The people of Mapungubwe built enclosures on hilltops, made pottery, herded cattle, and traded ivory and gold with the coastal ports 400 miles away. By the end of the 13th century, Mapungubwe had become an important center of political and economic power, one of a number of such regional centers in the interior of southeastern Africa.

Mapungubwe's influence expanded northward, across the Limpopo and onto the Zimbabwe Plateau. Here, people began building stone enclosures at new sites. After 1300, the center of political and economic power shifted from Mapungubwe to Zimbabwe. Some scholars think changes in the Indian Ocean trade may have caused the shift. Ivory had been Mapungubwe's main export and source of wealth, but evidence recovered from burials and trade ports suggests that the demand for gold began to grow. Ivory remained valuable, but gold was increasingly prized. The best sources of gold lay in the hills of the Zimbabwe Plateau, and Great Zimbabwe was closer to them than Mapungubwe. Mapungubwe began to decline as Great Zimbabwe's fortunes rose.

Great Zimbabwe was not an isolated urban center. It was the largest of 30 or 40 regional centers scattered across the plateau from the Kalahari Desert in the west and to the Indian Ocean lowlands in the east. Most of these centers shared Great

Found in the ruins of Mapungubwe, the kingdom that dominated the Limpopo River valley before Great Zimbabwe, this golden rhinoceros was most likely an emblem of royal power. To the Shona of modern Zimbabwe the rhinoceros is still a symbol of leadership.

Zimbabwe's distinctive architectural style, although none was as large, and they shared the same culture and economy. They were probably ruled from Great Zimbabwe by regional governors who collected tribute or taxes, in the form of gold and other goods, from the local people. In addition to these regional centers, the Zimbabwe civilization included many smaller settlements, from villages to single farmsteads.

In the 14th century, Great Zimbabwe controlled gold production on the Zimbabwe Plateau. The Zimbabweans had several methods of extracting gold. They panned for gold, sifting water and gravel from streambeds to obtain loose flakes and nuggets of gold that had been washed out of deposits of ore. The Zimbabweans also mined gold ore out of hard rock by digging horizontal, slanted, and vertical mineshafts, some reaching depths of more than 80 feet. Broken skeleton bones found in some of these shafts offer mute evidence that mining was a hazardous occupation.

Great Zimbabwe dominated the gold trade between the interior and Swahili ports such as Sofala on the eastern coast. The Swahili traders then shipped Zimbabwean gold to ports farther north along the coast. Among these was the great emporium, or trade center, at Kilwa. Arab traders from the Red Sea visited Kilwa, linking it to Egypt, the Mediterranean, Arabia, and the Near East, while Indian Ocean traders brought goods from as far away as China. The Swahili traders exchanged these imported goods for gold mined on the Zimbabwe Plateau.

The archaeological evidence shows that wealth was accumulated at Great Zimbabwe and that it was not evenly distributed among the population. Highly valued items such as gold and imported goods are found almost entirely inside the stone enclosures, rarely in the ruins

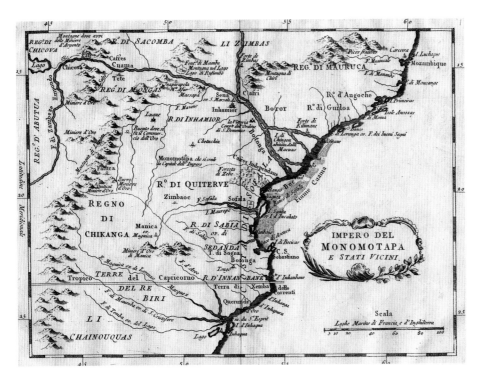

This 1781 map shows the empire of the powerful East African king Mono Motapa (or Mwene Mutapa), which included the states of Mapungubwe, Zimbabwe, and Mutapa. The Miniere d'Oro, or gold mines, were the foundation of the region's trade.

of outlying residences. The uneven distribution of wealth echoes other signs that society was divided into different classes. Houses outside the enclosures were smaller, less substantial, and more closely crowded together than those inside them. Cattle, especially young cattle, were eaten (or used in sacrificial rituals) inside the enclosures. In contrast, the diet of people living outside the enclosures consisted largely of sheep, goats, and game. In addition, Great Zimbabwe's long-distance trade and its large-scale building programs show that it was an organized state, not simply a large village.

Major construction at Great Zimbabwe seems to have ended around 1450. By that time, the quality of stonework had declined from its earlier high standard, and the city itself had begun to lose its importance as a center of trade and government. Archaeologists and historians have suggested several reasons for this decline. Great Zimbabwe was losing its importance in the trade network. Gold production was down—much of the easily obtainable gold had been stripped from the region, and areas to the north and west were becoming important as new sources of both copper and gold. But Great Zimbabwe's economy had been based on cattle before the rise of the gold trade. Why couldn't the city continue to thrive on a cattle-based economy? Some investigators think that the landscape could no longer support the city's large population. Huge herds of cattle had overgrazed the grasslands. Most nearby timber had been cut down. A series of droughts may have struck the area, increasing the stress on an already overburdened environment.

Whatever the reason, Great Zimbabwe declined in importance, probably slowly and over a century or longer. The Shona people of the region formed two new states, the successors to Great Zimbabwe. In the west was Torwa, whose capital city, Khami, had stone walls much like those of Great Zimbabwe. Some scholars think that the "square fortress, of masonry within and without, built of stones of marvelous size" that Portuguese historian João de Barros described in 1552 was Khami, not Great Zimbabwe. The other successor state, Rozwi, existed for many decades in and around the area of Great Zimbabwe.

The arrival of the Portuguese in East Africa in the 16th century brought instability to the Swahili coast and the Zimbabwe Plateau. After taking control of Kilwa in 1505, the Portuguese tried to take over the gold-trading routes to the interior. They never fully succeeded, but their efforts sparked resistance and war. Constant fighting and the rise of local warlords disrupted trade along routes that had been used for centuries. Ironically, the Portuguese search for

Symbol of a Nation

Zimbabwe is the only country in the world whose name is taken from an archaeological site. The stone birds of Great Zimbabwe appear on the national flag, the official seal, and the country's currency. Yet Great Zimbabwe's road to recognition as a national symbol has been a rocky one.

The careful work of archaeologists David Randall-MacIver and Gertrude Caton-Thompson should have done away with myths about Great Zimbabwe's origins early in the 20th century. For years, however, the white rulers of the country refused to accept the scientific evidence that black Africans had built Great Zimbabwe, the center of a powerful state. Since the late 19th century, the country that is now Zimbabwe had been known as Rhodesia, after the British industrialist Cecil Rhodes who had pioneered the white settlement and exploitation of the Shona homeland.

Land in Rhodesia was divided on a racial basis, with the country's white population controlling the best land and resources. With a strong interest in crushing any African liberation movements that arose in the country, Rhodesia's white government resisted the notion that black Africans had built Great Zimbabwe.

In the late 1960s, fighting broke out between the white government and groups such as the Zimbabwe African National Union (ZANU), which sought greater rights and powers for black Africans. The government responded by censoring books and articles about Great Zimbabwe and punishing scholars who published information and opinions about the site's African origins. A new government dominated by Rhodesia's black majority took control in 1980, however, and the country's name was changed to Zimbabwe in honor of the archaeological site that represents national and racial pride.

The glory of Great Zimbabwe is a proud symbol for the modern nation, which features the chevron bird on its flag. The carved soapstone bird also appears on the country's official seal and on its currency.

A late-20th-century artist painted this imagined scene of traders at Great Zimbabwe based on evidence from the site. The people wear Shona hairstyles, and the stone walls and the Conical Tower are in the background.

gold broke the links between the gold-producing interior and the coastal ports. The flow of wealth to the interior stopped. In the centuries that followed, the Shona people of the Zimbabwe Plateau suffered slave raids from the coast and invasions by African peoples from the south. Even before the arrival of the Portuguese, Great Zimbabwe's economic and political importance had faded. But during the centuries of turmoil the city was never entirely forgotten. The local people knew that the site had been the residence of powerful kings and chiefs in earlier times, and they continued to use it for religious rites, even after they turned some of its enclosures into cattle pens in the 19th century. Today, recognized as a major archaeological site and an emblem of African civilization, Great Zimbabwe has reclaimed its place in history.

Interview with Martin Hall

Rebecca Stefoff: David Randall-MacIver and Gertrude Caton-Thompson both concluded, based on good evidence, that Great Zimbabwe was built by Africans. How could so many people reject their evidence and their conclusions?

Martin Hall: Prejudice. People were so convinced that Africans were incapable of civilization that they weren't able to see the evidence in front of them. Even Gertrude Caton-Thompson was not free of prejudice. She argued that Great Zimbabwe must be African because the walls were circular—she believed that only "advanced" people built in straight lines. This prejudice continues in some quarters today—every now and again, someone suggests that Great Zimbabwe was built by early visitors from another continent, or that its origins are still a "mystery."

RS: What were some of the competing theories, both early in the 20th century and more recently?

MH: Earlier theories tended to be erratic or romantic. Some believed that Great Zimbabwe was built by wandering Arab

Archaeologist Martin Hall (top) and writer Rebecca Stefoff (bottom).

tribes. Others saw the hand of the Queen of Sheba, or the mythical Prester John—a fabulously wealthy Christian king living deep in Africa, or perhaps in Asia. More recent debates have been far more sober, and have focused on the origins of the people who lived at Great Zimbabwe, and on what the buildings were used for. Some archaeologists believe that there was cultural continuity between the farming communities who settled the Zimbabwe Plateau early in the present era and the Great Zimbabweans. Others have argued that Great Zimbabwe's cultural links were to the south, as communities crossed the Limpopo River in search of new economic opportunities. There has also been a good deal of discussion about what the buildings were used for, particularly the Great Enclosure. What is certain, though, is that this was a place of great cultural and political significance in a major precolonial society.

RS: What effects have this controversy had on political life in Rhodesia, now Zimbabwe?

MH: When the country was Rhodesia, the white minority regime hated the idea that Great Zimbabwe was built by black people, and tried hard to suppress this suggestion. One leading archaeologist was hounded from the country, and the regime supported crackpot interpretations that would support the idea of inherent white superiority. Not surprisingly, Great Zimbabwe became an important cultural symbol for the liberation movement, and a rallying point for the nation's new identity. Others have put forward bizarre theories of an idyllic, precolonial black society, in which everyone lived in a state of nature, free from exploitation—a sort of black Eldorado. This is improbable. Great Zimbabwe was the center of a state in which there was clearly inequality and exploitation. Overall, though, it's hardly surprising that there should be such controversies. Important archaeological sites such as these are important cultural and political symbols, and we should expect them to generate controversy.

RS: If a new round of active excavation were to begin at Great Zimbabwe, what would you like to investigate? Where would you dig, and what would you look for?

MH: We still know so little about everyday life at Great Zimbabwe—about how ordinary people lived, what they ate, the crafts in which they specialized, how households were made up. Modern archaeology has made great advances in deducing the nature of the everyday economy, gender relations, and how people marked their identities through clothes and ornaments. There is still the potential to investigate aspects such as these at Great Zimbabwe—a wonderful challenge for archaeologists in the future.

Glossary

archaeozoology The study of animal life found at or near archaeological sites, focusing on the role animals played in the life of the site's inhabitants.

artifact An object made by humans such as a tool, weapon, utensil, or artwork.

celadon Pale-green pottery made in China.

chevron V-shaped pattern.

courses In stonework, the rows or layers of stones making up a wall.

dhaka Mixture of clay and gravel used for building.

dhow Ship with triangular sails, used for hundreds of years in the Indian Ocean.

drought Prolonged period of reduced rainfall; if severe, a drought can destroy crops, leading to famine.

ethnography The recording and study of the ways in which human cultures express themselves, such as rituals, music, and mythology; comparative ethnography examines the ways in which cultures are different or similar.

exfoliation Process in which temperature changes cause layers of rock to split and separate.

inscription Wording or symbols on an artifact or structure.

madzimbabwe Stone enclosures.

masonry Stonework or brickwork.

monolith Standing pillar, tower, or rock.

mortar Material such as cement or plaster used to hold stonework in place in construction.

oral tradition Elements of culture passed from generation to generation through the spoken word rather than in writing; a culture's oral tradition may include folk tales, sayings, songs, and more.

organic matter A mass of living (or once-living) material, including hair, leather, blood, cloth, pottery, wood, and bone.

potsherd Fragment of broken pottery.

sheikh Title of a chieftain or leader in an Arab or Arab-influenced community, such as a tribe or city.

soapstone Soft, easily carved stone, usually gray-green and slick to the touch, containing talc, chlorite and, magnetite.

stratigraphy Method of studying and dating archaeological sites according to the depth of various layers, or strata, of soil and buried relics and debris. The general rule of stratigraphy is: the deeper the stratum, the older the material.

thatch Roofing made of plant material, such as straw.

tribute Payment in money or goods made, sometimes under threat of force, by a population to a ruler or by a less powerful nation to a more powerful one.

Great Zimbabwe and Related Sites

GREAT ZIMBABWE NATIONAL MONUMENT

www.zimheritage.co.zw/site/ sr_gzim.htm

The Great Zimbabwe National Monument was designated a UNESCO World Heritage site and the Zimbabwean government made it a national monument. Located approximately 18 miles from the town of Masvingo, and 180 miles south

of Harare, the site covers an area of nearly 1,800 acres. Great Zimbabwe is one of the most extensive and best-preserved ruins anywhere in Africa south of the Sahara Desert.

K2 (BAMBANDYANALO)

A small village situated at the foot of Bambandyanalo Hill in South Africa, K2 is .60 miles southwest of Mapungubwe Hill in a valley surrounded by cliffs. G. A. Gardner, who excavated there during the 1930s, named it K2. Between about 1030 and 1220 CE, many generations of farmers lived at K2. The main site includes the remains of a central homestead area, a cattle *kraal* (central space for cattle), and a central midden (refuse heap) surrounded by smaller homesteads.

KHAMI RUINS NATIONAL MONUMENT

www.worldheritagesite.org/sites/ khamiruins.html

Recognized as a World Heritage Site, the Khami Ruins National Monument is located in the western region of Zimbabwe.

On the banks of a river with the same name, Khami was the capital of the Torwa state. Built in the 15th century, the buildings of Khami have their own distinctive stone architecture, a combination of house platforms and low, freestanding walls that are often intricately decorated with checkered and herringbone patterns.

KILWA

Kilwa, a town on the east coast of Africa, was an important trading partner with Great Zimbabwe beginning in the 12th century. From the 10th to the late 15th centuries, Kilwa was a prosperous Islamic coastal city, dominated by a mosque and houses built from blocks of coral, with a population estimated at between 4,000 and 12,000 people. Today, visitors can see the remnants of a palace, prison, two mosques, and other buildings overlooking the Kilwa port.

MANYIKENI

Manyikeni is a good example of an outlying Zimbabwe settlement. It is located about 250 miles east of the high Zimbabwe Plateau and 31 miles away from Vilankulos Bay on the Indian Ocean. Here, despite the lack of materials to build in the style of Great Zimbabwe, there are the familiar architectural features.

MAPUNGUBWE CULTURAL LANDSCAPE
www.mapungubwe.com

Mapungubwe, on the Limpopo River, preceded Great Zimbabwe as a center of power on the Zimbabwe Plateau. Occupied primarily in the 12th century, Mapungubwe is widely known for the rich goods found in its graves, particularly for a small, gold rhinoceros found in a grave excavated in 1932. A symbol of the Mapungubwe king's power, the golden rhino is considered one of South Africa's most important national treasures. Located about 283 miles north of the city of Pretoria in South

Africa, the Mapungubwe Cultural Landscape is recognized as a UNESCO World Heritage Site.

NENGA AND PAMUUYA
Nenga and PaMuuya are good examples of smaller *madzimbabwe*, or stone houses. These two sites are on the southwestern margins of the Zimbabwe Plateau, where the Lundi River flows toward its junction with the Sabi River. With only one and two stone enclosures respectively, these were small regional power centers. Their architecture is similar to that of Great Zimbabwe.

Further Reading

Bessire, Mark. *Great Zimbabwe.* New York: Franklin Watts, 1998.

Editors of Time-Life Books. *Africa's Glorious Legacy.* Alexandria, Va.: Time-Life Books, 1994.

Garlake, Peter S. *Great Zimbabwe.* London: Thames and Hudson, 1973.

————. *Life at Great Zimbabwe.* Gweru, Zimbabwe: Mambo Press, 1982.

Garner, David. "The Heart of an Empire." *Geographical Magazine,* August 1996, 40–41.

Huffman, Thomas N. *Symbols in Stone: Unravelling the Mystery of Great Zimbabwe.* Johannesburg, South Africa: University of Witwatersrand Press, 1987.

————. *Mapungubwe: Ancient African Civilisations of the Limpopo.* Johannesburg, South Africa: Wits University Press, 2005.

Martin, David. *Great Zimbabwe: Houses of Stone.* Harare, Zimbabwe: African Publishing Group, 1998.

McIntosh, Roderick J. "Riddle of Great Zimbabwe." *Archaeology,* July/August 1998, 44–49.

Ndoro, Webber. "Great Zimbabwe." *Scientific American,* November 1997, 94–99.

Tyson, Peter. "Mystery of Great Zimbabwe," *NOVA Online* (November 2000). www.pbs.org/wgbh/nova/israel/zimbabwe.html.

Index

Martin Hall is a historical archaeologist who has researched and written about the first farming communities of southern Africa, the origins of complex societies, and the archaeology of colonial settlement. He worked in Kwa-Zulu Natal, South Africa, before joining the University of Cape Town as professor of historical archaeology. He has published more than one hundred papers and several books, and served as the president of the World Archaeological Congress. He is now deputy vice chancellor of the University of Cape Town.

Rebecca Stefoff is the author of many books for young readers. History and science are among her favorite subjects. She has previously written about archaeology in *Finding the Lost Cities* and *The Palace of Minos at Knossos*, another book in this series.

Brian Fagan is professor of anthropology at the University of California, Santa Barbara. He is internationally known for his books on archaeology, among them *The Adventure of Archaeology*, *The Rape of the Nile*, *Archaeologists: Explorers of the Human Past*, and *The Oxford Companion to Archaeology*.

digging
for the past

Sites in This Series

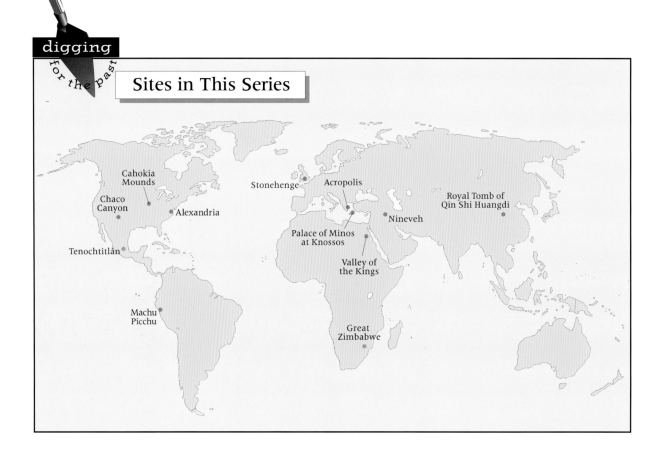